IMAGES
of England

BURY FOOTBALL CLUB

There was a magnificent feeling of pride in evidence all around Gigg Lane as David Pugh and Chris Lucketti raised the Division Two trophy high on 3 May 1997.

IMAGES
of England

BURY FOOTBALL CLUB

Compiled by
Peter Cullen

TEMPUS

First published 1998
Copyright © Peter Cullen, 1998

Tempus Publishing Limited
The Mill, Brimscombe Port,
Stroud, Gloucestershire, GL5 2QG

ISBN 0 7524 1526 3

Typesetting and origination by
Tempus Publishing Limited
Printed in Great Britain by
Midway Clark Printing, Wiltshire

Present and forthcoming titles by Tempus Publishing:

Bristol Rovers Football Club
Bury Football Club
Cardiff City Football Club 1899-1947
Cardiff City Football Club 1947-1971
Charlton Athletic Football Club
Crystal Palace Football Club
Exeter City Football Club 1904-1994
Newport County Football Club 1912-1960
Plymouth Argyle Football Club 1886-1986
Reading Football Club
Sheffield United Football Club
Sunderland Football Club
Swansea Town Football Club 1912-1964
Tranmere Rovers Football Club

Contents

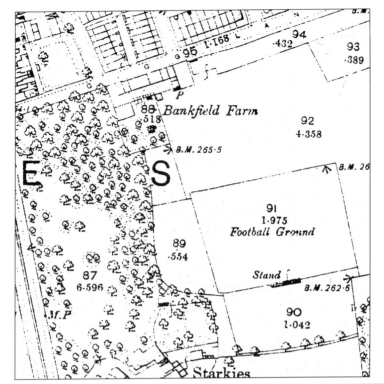

The 1890 Ordnance Survey map of the Fishpool area of Bury, shows Bury Football Club's Gigg Lane home as yet very much undeveloped, with just a small covered stand on the south side of the ground. The site had become Bury's home upon their formation on 24 April 1885, when they became tenants of one of Lord Derby's fields.

The 1910 Ordnance Survey map shows much development has taken place, with three covered stands now running the length of the north, south and east sides of the ground. Only the Manchester Road end remains uncovered. Notice how the Bankfield Farm buildings have now spread along Gigg Lane, with the entrance to the ground being through a gate almost directly opposite Brierley Street.

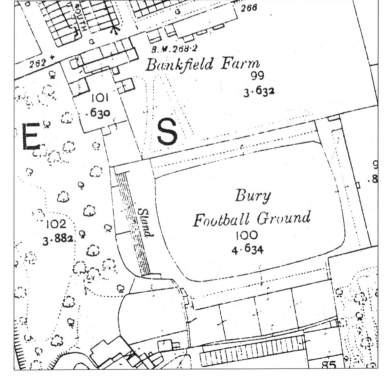

The author and his wife outside Wembley.

Introduction

If, on the spur of the moment, a football fan was asked to name any north-west football club – *Family Fortunes* style – it would be fair to say that Bury Football Club would probably be way down on most people's list. 'Where exactly is Bury?' I have been asked on several occasions during my travels with the Shakers over the past quarter of a century and, even worse, 'Is Bury in Yorkshire?'

In fact, many 'outsiders' seem to be completely oblivious to the past glories and successful early history of Bury Football Club – much of it at the very top level of domestic football. It is a small-town Lancashire club (we'll never accept that we are now supposed to be in Greater Manchester), which has enjoyed major triumphs during its first fifty or so years of existence and had survived for seventy-one years in Divisions One and Two before finally falling into the dreaded lower divisions in 1956 (admittedly after a few earlier reprieves). The club has had two FA Cup Final wins, numerous international players on its books and twenty-two seasons in the top flight (including final League positions of fourth and fifth in the old Division One during the glorious 1920s). Undoubtedly, the post-war years have been more modest but, although the club struggled for its very existence on three occasions in the 1970s, 1980s and 1990s, we've still had our moments and have bounced back to a healthy position in recent years.

I'm a firm believer in supporting your local town club. I have always done so and always will do. If Bury did ever cease to exist, I doubt whether I would be able to transfer my allegiance to any other team. It's strange how a club can get a hold and completely hook you – but I suppose I'm just one of many thousands of people at many different clubs over the past century or so to be affected in such a way!

Born in Bury, I've always lived in the town and there was a great tradition of watching the Shakers in my family. I suppose that I carried that tradition on – but on a greater scale! At first, it was just attending the home games, then, during the relative success under the management of Bob Smith in the 1970s, things snowballed and I began to attend away matches. Going to every game became a must, with the thrill of visiting new grounds and the need to collect each match programme. A spell followed as the secretary of Bury FC Supporters' Association, various roles on fund-raising committees during the 1980s and nine years as programme editor. Then, in 1997, with Bury happily back in Division One, a surprise call from commercial manager, Nev Neville, brought the chance to work for the club full-time as ticket manager and programme editor. I suppose that I had served my apprenticeship, but it was still a totally unexpected opportunity and one that I was delighted to accept.

As the club's official historian, I compiled a centenary brochure for the club in 1985 and, surprisingly, there has not been another publication featuring Bury FC until this photographic history. I am hoping to one day publish a full statistical history of the club.

I am extremely grateful for the kindness and co-operation of many like-minded supporters who have allowed me access to their own photographs, scrapbooks and memorabilia and assisted me greatly in the compilation of this book. I offer my sincere thanks to the *Bury Times*, *Bolton Evening News* and *Manchester Evening News* for their assistance with photographs, along with Joan Curtis, John Dawson, Les Deegan, Harry Driver, Dawn Ellison, Paul Greenlees, Joy Hart, Eric Massey, Jack Smith, Dave Willitts and anyone else I may have neglected to mention. I must thank my wife, Sue, for her patience (sometimes) while I collated and wrote these pages, week after week and was totally anti-social. Thanks also to James Howarth and the staff at Tempus Publishing for their assistance and advice.

I can't hide my fascination for Bury Football Club, its history, personalities past and present and, of course, wonderful Gigg Lane. I know that the club also plays a big part in many other people's lives and I hope the reader will find this pictorial history both fascinating and informative.

Peter Cullen
October 1998

One
Early Successes

Bury's line-up of 1887 shows the players in their chocolate and blue halved shirts, just two years after the club's formation. From left to right, back row: Tom Hargreaves (Secretary), J. Robinson, A. Ghent, J. Wright, J.A. Ross, F. Wright, J. Ward, J. Hoyle. Front Row: W. Pollock, J. Clark, A. Malpass, G. Douglas, W. Lee. On the ground: H. Hitchen and A. Howarth.

Bury FC unveils its first covered stand, built on the south side of Gigg Lane in 1887, at a cost of £50 11s 8d. The stand was opened on 5 November, when a crowd of 2,000 witnessed a 4-1 win against Heywood in the Lancashire Junior Cup First Round.

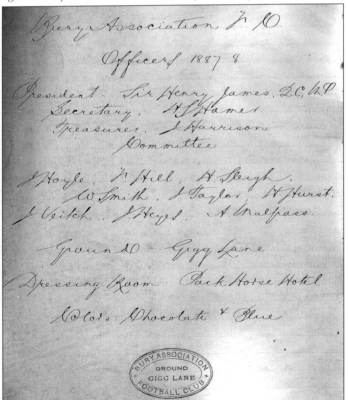

The opening page from the committee minute book, from August 1887, stating the club's elected officers. The famous Sir Henry James is named as the president, the Pack Horse Hotel (a public house on nearby Parkhills Road) as the dressing room – with no changing facilities yet available at Gigg Lane – and the club's distinctive chocolate and blue colours confirmed. It wasn't until 1888 that Bury first commenced playing in their famous white shirts and blue shorts.

Bury are on the attack towards the Cemetery End of Gigg Lane in this game, which took place in the late 1880s. The 'terracing' consisted of six raised planks of wood, whilst a number of fans also chose to perch precariously on the rear boundary wall.

The grandstand and paddock (on the site of the present day Main Stand) are full to bursting as Bury – helped by a celebrity kick-off from the Mayor – commence a Lancashire Junior Cup Quarter-final replay against local rivals Heywood Central on 8 February 1890. The 9,000 crowd witnessed a 4-1 Bury win. The houses on the right are the terraced houses that still stand on Gigg Lane.

The Lancashire Senior Cup was a prestigious tournament when Bury first entered the competition in the 1891/92 season, but the trophy was captured at the first attempt. Bury knocked out Newton Heath, Accrington and Everton, eventually beating Blackburn Rovers 2-0 in the final at Preston. It was in this game that the Bury chairman, J.T. Ingham, pronounced Bury to be 'The Shakers' for the first time. From left to right, back row: Pemberton, Jobson, Warburton, Lowe, Cooper, Ross. Front row: Wilkinson, Spence, Conway, Bourne, Plant.

Complete with a bench perched upon two buckets, trouser belt, cravat and trainer's towel, this is the Shakers team that finished second in the Lancashire League in the 1893/94 season and gained election to the Division Two of the Football League. There are some famous names amongst the line-up of, from left to right, back row: Barbour, McNaughton, Lowe, Clegg, Davies, Ross, Mills. Front row: Wyllie, Barr, Millar, Lee, Plant.

The club's first season in the Football League, in 1894/95, ended with the clinching of the Division Two championship and a home record which read 'played fifteen, won fifteen'. These were the lads who achieved the feat. From left to right, back row: Barbour, Montgomery, Holmes, Davidson, Davies, Wardle (Chairman). Middle row: Bradley, Graham, Pray, Clegg, Ross, Broome. Front row: Wyllie, Barr, Millar, Henderson, Plant.

Early photos of Gigg Lane remain incredibly scarce for some reason, despite the club's elevated position in Division One at the turn of the twentieth century. Although somewhat unclear, Gigg Lane is seen here in 1897, looking from the Manchester Road End of the ground towards the South Stand side, with the Cemetery End in the distance.

Bury Football Club celebrated the turn of a new century by lifting the FA Cup, for the first time, in the 1899/1900 season. The Shakers beat Southampton 4-0 in the final – played on 21 April 1900 in front of a crowd of 68,945 at the Crystal Palace – despite being considered as underdogs. From left to right, back row: Darroch, Thompson, Davidson. Middle row: Fairhurst (Trainer), Pray, Leeming, Ross, Wardle (Chairman). Front row: Richards, Wood, McLuckie, Sagar, Plant.

George Ross, the son of a Scottish police sergeant based in Lancashire, joined Bury in 1886 and first played for the club on 26 February 1887 – less than two years after the club's formation. By the time he left Bury Football Club, an amazing twenty years later, he had amassed 367 Football League appearances, plus a further 200-odd Lancashire League and friendly appearances during the pre-League days. He had won a Division Two championship medal, two FA Cup-winners medals and spent eleven years playing in Division One. He was truly one of Bury's greatest-ever players.

The 1900 FA Cup Final. Jack Pray takes a throw-in and aims for centre forward Charlie Sagar. The officials look like they are out for a Sunday stroll, but the game turned into something of a stroll for Bury.

Jack Plant leaves his man grounded as he races towards goal in the 1900 FA Cup Final against Southampton.

Saints 'keeper Robinson dives in vain as William Wood's shot registers the second goal for Bury.

Already 3-0 ahead, the Shakers kick-off at the start of the second half.

Jack Plant again beats his man on that magnificent afternoon at the Crystal Palace.

A moment to savour, as Bury captain Jack Pray receives the FA Cup from Sir Henry James, the Bury president, on 21 April 1900. This was the club's first major success.

Bury playing a Division One away game at Villa Park against Aston Villa on 11 January 1902. The Shakers face a corner here with (from left to right) 'keeper Fred Thompson, full-backs Joe Leeming and Jock McEwan and centre half Frank Thorpe all alert to the danger. However, after a goal-less first half, Villa eventually won 2-0.

In the same game, at a very wet Villa Park, William Wood (far left) passes the ball out to the wing, watched by fellow Shaker Frank Thorpe. The referee's attire is particularly interesting in this image!

Bury's defence of the FA Cup in 1901 began with a 1-0 away win at Sheffield Wednesday, but brought defeat in the Second Round, losing 2-1 away against Southern League Tottenham Hotspur. Left-winger Jack Plant is seen here, forcing a save out of the Spurs 'keeper.

The Spurs 'keeper, Cawley, fists out a Bury shot. It is interesting to note that he is sporting the same striped shirt as his outfield colleagues.

Bury are back at the Crystal Palace on 18 April 1903, as they reach the FA Cup Final for the second time inside three years. This time, Derby County are the opponents and Bury appeared in an all-blue kit, allowing the Rams to wear their usual white shirts. Although Bury ran out 6-0 winners, the photographer managed to capture a rare moment of Bury defence.

Captain George Ross collected the famous trophy for Bury as captain and George's medal from the 1903 success has happily survived the test of time.

This is how the *Daily Despatch* saw Bury's triumphant homecoming in 1903.

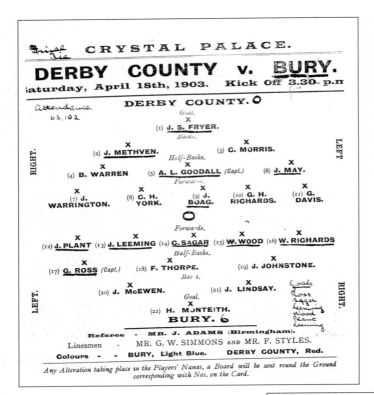

CRYSTAL PALACE.

DERBY COUNTY v. BURY.
Saturday, April 18th, 1903. Kick Off 3.30 p.m

Attendance. 63,102

DERBY COUNTY. 0

Goal.
X
(1) **J. S. FRYER.**
Backs.

RIGHT.

X (2) **J. METHVEN.**　　　　　X (3) **C. MORRIS.**

LEFT.

Half-Backs.
X (4) **B. WARREN**　　X (5) **A. L. GOODALL** (Capt.)　　X (6) **J. MAY.**

Forwards.
X (7) **J. WARRINGTON.**　X (8) **G. H. YORK.**　X (9) **J. BOAG.**　X (10) **G. H. RICHARDS.**　X (11) **G. DAVIS.**

O

Forwards.
X (12) **J. PLANT**　(13) **J. LEEMING**　X (14) **G. SAGAR**　(15) **W. WOOD**　X (16) **W. RICHARDS**

Half-Backs.
X (17) **G. ROSS** (Capt.)　X (18) **F. THORPE.**　X (19) **J. JOHNSTONE.**

LEFT.

Bacs.
X (20) **J. McEWEN.**　　X (21) **J. LINDSAY.**

RIGHT.

Goals
Ross
Sagar
Leeming
Wood
Plant
Leeming

Goal.
X (22) **H. MONTEITH.**

BURY. 6

Referee - **MR. J. ADAMS** (Birmingham).
Linesmen - MR. G. W. SIMMONS AND MR. F. STYLES.
Colours - - **BURY, Light Blue.**　**DERBY COUNTY, Red.**

Any Alteration taking place in the Players' Names, a Board will be sent round the Ground corresponding with Nos. on the Card.

This match programme for Bury's 1903 thrashing of Derby County shows the 6-0 scoreline, which still remains a record FA Cup Final winning margin almost a century later. The programme is obviously much sought after by collectors – and is probably worth at least £3,000 today.

To mark the achievement of winning the 1903 FA Cup without conceding a single goal during the five games played, the Bury directors had an attractive gold medal struck for each player involved in the cup run.

Bury's record-breaking, 1903 FA Cup-winning squad. From left to right, back row: J. Johnston, J. Lindsay, F. Thorpe, H. Monteith, G. Ross, ? McEwan. Front row: W. Richards, W. Wood, C. Sagar, J. Leeming, J. Plant.

Bury Football Club enjoyed a good year in 1903, capturing the FA Cup, Lancashire Cup and Manchester Cup.

Centre forward Charlie Sagar was the very first in a long line of players that Bury have been forced to part with over the years, simply in order to balance the books. Sagar joined Bury from Turton in 1898 and played 186 League games, scoring seventy goals over the next seven years. He also became the club's first international player, when he was capped twice for England.

Goalkeeper Archie Montgomery was Bury's regular goalkeeper from 1895 to 1906, appearing in 210 League games – but he missed both FA Cup Finals. In August 1907, he was eventually appointed as the club's very first secretary/manager, but the First World War led to Archie's departure, as the club set about greatly reducing expenditure.

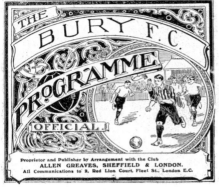

Price One Penny.)   (Copyright. Entered at Stationer's Hall.

SATURDAY, DECEMBER 11th, 1909.

THE BURY F.C. PROGRAMME
OFFICIAL

Proprietor and Publisher by Arrangement with the Club
ALLEN GREAVES, SHEFFIELD & LONDON.
All Communications to 2, Red Lion Court, Fleet St., London E.C.

THE DERBY HOTEL,
MARKET STREET, BURY.
THE COMMERCIAL HOTEL.
LUNCHEON · ONE O'CLOCK DAILY.
Hot Teas ready on conclusion of Match.

Telephone No 0230.   FRANK J. CAIN, Proprietor.

The committee and directors' minute books mention 'official cards' in the 1890s and 'programmes' in the early 1900s, although the earliest known Bury programme is an issue from 11 December 1909, when Bury defeated Chelsea 4-2 at Gigg Lane. It is a sixteen-page issue, priced at one penny with a pale green cover. The London publishers Allen Greaves produced it on behalf of the club.

W. HIBBERT. BURY. F.C.

Billy Hibbert was perhaps Bury's last pre-First World War star. A nimble centre forward, and slight of build, Hibbert joined Bury from Bryn Central in May 1906 and, over a five-year period, scored ninety-nine League goals in 178 games for the Shakers. He was also capped for England in 1910 and went on the FA tour of South Africa the same year. When he signed for Newcastle in October 1911, the fee of £1,950 was a British record transfer amount at the time.

Two
Between the Wars

Bury's players and officials line up in solemn mood at the Cenotaph in London, where captain William Peake lays a wreath in memory of the war dead – and especially ex-Shaker Teddy Bullen. A policeman has also joined the group.

For the first two seasons directly after the First World War, Bury were forced to change their registered colours from their famous white shirts and blue shorts, simply because of the scarcity of materials. Between 1919 and 1921, Bury turned out in red-and-white hooped shirts and dark blue shorts. Scottish left-back, John 'Jock' Allen, is modelling the kit here in Bury's away fixture at Fulham on 22 January 1921 – a game which ended 0-0. A player at Bury since 1913, Allen played 132 games for the Shakers up until 1922, but was subsequently banned for life by the FA for match fixing.

Teddy Bullen was the only player on the club's books to be killed in action during the First World War when he fell at Vaux on 11 August 1917. For many years, this brass plaque stood in the Gigg Lane boardroom as a tribute to a brave soldier and a fine club servant. Teddy was a left half-back who played 188 League games for the Shakers, having joined the club from Altrincham in May 1906.

It seems that Bury's players were happy to accept any request from a photographer – no matter how silly! In 1921, Burkinshaw, Callagher, McCrae, Smith, Robbie and Hird suddenly decided to take up smoking clay pipes. The event was probably staged for the benefit of the *Topical Times*.

Some things don't change it seems, even if footballers' fashion sense does. Golf remains a popular sport for footballers today and the Shakers players of 1922, looking particularly smart in collars and ties, are set for a day on the golf course. From left to right: Porter, Gray, Adamson, Burkinshaw, Lomas, Cook, Robbie, Perry, Callagher, Cornthwaite, Aitkin, Plunkett, Andrews, Stage, McCrae and Yates.

Still on the golf course in 1922 and John Callagher, Bob Perry and Jock Aitken are obviously enjoying themselves.

A Scotsman, James Hunter Thomson – better known as 'Jimmy' – played for Hearts, Leith, Portsmouth, Bury and Nelson before returning to Gigg Lane as assistant to William Cameron in 1922. An important appointment in June 1923 saw him named as Cameron's successor and Thomson remained Bury's secretary/manager until 1927. During that time, he guided the club to promotion into Division One in his first season, masterminded the redevelopment of Gigg Lane in 1924 and helped the club obtain its best-ever final placing in 1926 – fourth in Division One.

A glimpse of Gigg Lane, before its massive redevelopment of 1924. The stand to the left is the original Main Stand from the 1890s, with the old Cemetery End stand in the distance. Preseason fun in 1923 meant a tug-o'-war, which was no doubt just for the benefit of the camera. From left to right: Robbie, Bradshaw, Ball, Plunkett, Perry, Richardson, Callagher, Cornthwaite, unknown, Yates.

The stumps are ready for the action to begin in 1923. The bat is believed to be a French cricket bat and appears to be the subject of much frivolity. Notice the goalposts in the background on what was, prior to 1924, a training pitch on the site of the current car park. Gigg Lane is in the background, but there are no turnstiles showing yet. From left to right: Robbie, Callagher, Cornthwaite, Thompson, Plunkett, Ball, Richardson.

Finishing runners-up behind Leeds United in the 1923/24 season, Bury were promoted to Division One for a second stint after mounting a strong finish during the closing months of the campaign. From left to right, back row: Yates (Trainer), Wood (Director), Adamson, Brown (Director), Richardson, Savery, Fairhurst (Checker), unknown, Fox, Paine (Secretary), Day (Asst Trainer). Third Row: Whittam, Robinson (Director), Seymour, Longworth (Director), Davies, Duckworth (Chairman), Robbie, Hamer (Financial Secretary), Stevenson, Unsworth (Director). Second Row: Thomson (Manager), Brooks, Smith, Heap, Stage, Bradshaw, Butler, Finney, Porter, Sandiford (Director). Front Row: Humpish, Matthews, Bullock, Ball, Amos, Ward, Turner, Plunkett.

A view towards the back of the Main Stand from the Manchester Road side of the old training pitch – which is by now strewn with debris and building materials. Much of the 1897 rear-stand wall remained buried under the newly-built structure of 1924, but was re-discovered in 1992, when further ground developments took place.

The redevelopment of 1924 involved the Main Stand and South sides of the ground. In mid-July, the Main Stand roof has been demolished and a rail track laid in the Paddock, in order to assist with removal of debris and earth. Notice how high above the pitch the Paddock originally was. The 'old' frontage of the 1897 stand remained an integral part of the extended 1924 stand.

A view that will be familiar to many fans, as work continues on completing the 'new' Main Stand in August 1924. Only days remained before the Shakers were due to take on Manchester City at Gigg Lane and still the roof was incomplete, the back and side walls missing and most of the 5,600 bench seats needed fitting! The 'striped' portion of the front wall is the old stand showing through, whilst the majority is still bare unpainted wood.

Gigg Lane opens its new turnstiles on 30 August 1924 for the first time, as a (then) record 33,523 crowd descends on the redeveloped ground for the visit of Manchester City. Not quite everything is finished, the Main Stand has no window frames fitted yet, many seats were also missing and there are still building materials – instead of cars – covering the intended new car park. City spoilt the party as well by winning 2-0.

Tom 'Tiny' Bradshaw shares a joke in training with Jack Ball and trainer Alf Yates in 1927. The following year, Bradshaw became Bury's first and only Scottish international capped player, whilst, also in 1928, Ball earned his solitary England cap against Northern Ireland.

A spot of leap-frog training for half-back Alec Robinson (in the air) and Henry Dutton in 1927. Robinson played 126 League games for Bury between 1926 and 1933, when he earned a £5,000 transfer to Burnley. He later returned to the club in a coaching position and also played for the Bury Shakers baseball team at Gigg in 1936. Dutton had cost a sizeable £1,300 when signed from West Brom, but only remained at the club one season.

High spirits in training in 1927 as joker Billy Stage (second left) leads the way, accompanied by Jack Ball, Tom Adamson and Wally Amos.

A spot of cards for Joe Hughes, Sam Wynne, George Brooks and Arthur Finney, watched by their colleagues. Right-back Wynne joined Bury for £2,250 from Oldham in December 1926, but, tragically, collapsed and died during Bury's away game at Sheffield United in April 1927.

The reason for the black arm-bands is uncertain, but Billy Stage and Norman Bullock certainly look solemn as the brass band plays in the background at Gigg Lane during the 1920s.

Norman Bullock spent his entire playing career with the Shakers between 1920 and 1935. For almost half-a-century, he held the club records for most career League goals (124) and most goals in a season (34). He still retains the record for most League appearances – playing in 506 matches. Two spells as manager and three England caps whilst at Bury make Norman Bullock one of the club's major personalities.

There were no apprentices to clean their boots for them in 1927, so Bury's Division One stars set about the job themselves in the entrance to the tunnel. From left to right: David Robbie, Billy Harrison, Tom Bradshaw, Joe Hughes, Tommy Chester, Jimmy Chambers and Arthur Finney. There was obviously much camaraderie between the players.

A day to savour for Bury on 14 September 1931 – and especially David Robbie – as Bury hammer Barnsley 7-1 at Gigg Lane, with the right-winger grabbing four of the goals. Robbie (partially hidden) is seen here claiming one of his four successful strikes.

Robbie, Stage, Bullock, Ball and Amos – that was Bury's famed and successful forward line for much of the 1920s. The two wingers in question, Robbie and Amos, demonstrate the difference in their respective heights as they smile for the camera at a sunny Gigg Lane.

Wally Amos stood at just a shade over 5' 4" tall, but for twelve years he terrorised the opposition down Bury's left wing. Amos cost £350 when he signed from Worksop Town in May 1923, but he proved to be a bargain, as he went on to play in 479 League and cup games for the Shakers, scoring 132 goals. In the 1950s, he returned to Bury as assistant trainer.

A happy and informal team gathering at the end of the tunnel in 1927. Alex Massie and Tom Bradshaw (far left), both went on to become Scotland internationals – Bradshaw with the Shakers and Massie later gaining eighteen caps with Hearts and Aston Villa. Goalkeeper Billy Richardson (with cap) is obviously the joker in the pack.

David Robbie was the supplier and scorer of many goals for the Shakers from his right-wing position between 1921 and 1934. The balding Scotsman played in 420 League games for the club and scored 102 goals, which takes him to sixth place in Bury's list of all-time scorers.

When Jimmy Thomson resigned as manager in 1927, the Shakers turned to Nelson boss Percy Smith as his successor. During his time at Gigg Lane, Bury were relegated from Division One and sold Tiny Bradshaw to Liverpool for £8,250. He left in January 1930, and gained much success at Tottenham before managing Notts County and Bristol Rovers.

Christmas Day 1930 and director Charley Dean officially presented the club with a new billiards room. Here, the players of 1932 are watching Alec Robinson attempt a trick-shot. The same room and table remained at Gigg Lane until the mid-1980s, when corporate hospitality dictated that the room became a sponsors' lounge. From left to right: Porter, Grass, Chester, Smith, Robbie, Bullock, Gemmell, Mills, Robinson, Amos, Lindsay.

John Reid Smith had enjoyed a glittering career by the time he landed at Bury in March 1928. He was a Scottish FA Cup winner with Kilmarnock in 1920, had scored a goal in the first-ever Wembley FA Cup Final (for Bolton who won 2-0 in 1923) and notched a total of eighty-seven goals for the Trotters. The £1,500 that Bury paid for him was a bargain, as Smith scored a hat-trick on his debut and, over the following six years, grabbed 108 goals for the club in just 157 games. Not a bad ratio!

Guess which magazine persuaded this bunch to pose for the camera in the early 1930s!

Bury played Swansea Town at Gigg Lane on 9 January 1932 in an FA Cup Third Round tie and, due to a clash of colours, appeared in an unfamiliar all-red kit. 13,268 watched Bury beat the Welshmen – David Robbie surges forward here – and the Shakers went on to eventually reach the Sixth Round.

Wally Amos scores Bury's second goal in a 4-3 defeat by Manchester City at Gigg Lane in the FA Cup Sixth Round in 1932. The crowd of 28,035 that day was treated to a classic, as Bury went 3-0 down and fought back, only to lose by the narrowest of margins – we've never reached that stage in the FA Cup since.

A free header for David Robbie as he scores the winner against Burnley on 5 March 1932 in front of a surprisingly low crowd of 8,517. The Burnley manager won't have been happy with his defence!

Plymouth 'keeper Harry Cann gathers the ball from Robbie and O'Rourke (who made a scoring debut) in this 2-1 win on 13 October 1932. Notice the absence of numbers on the shirts still.

Tall tales from David Robbie with Billy Chalmers, Billy Whitfield and Arthur Buttery.

Sammy Earl, Alf Edmunds and Arthur Buttery all await treatment in 1933.

A touch of study in 1934, when Bury became one of the first clubs to introduce a library for the players at the ground (in the Billiards Room). From left to right: Archie Dowall, Billy Harrison, Leslie Vernon, David Robbie, Sammy Earl. *Life's What You Make It* is the title of Sammy's book!

Gigg Lane in the 1930s was an impressive sight, despite the terracing on three sides consisting simply of earth mounds. The Manchester Road End is not yet covered and the Cemetery End roof has another couple of decades to go before being blown off in a gale. Chief scout Jimmy Porter, in later years, used to produce this photograph for effect when trying to sign up promising youngsters.

There seems to have been a club cat adopted at Gigg Lane, even since the earliest days at the turn of the century, and there remains one today. Alec Robinson and J.R. Smith show a little affection in 1933.

Player/manager Norman Bullock discusses team tactics in 1935, improvising with pawns from a chess set. From left to right: Gemmell, Robbie, Tremelling, Self, Whitfield, Bell, Bullock, Buttery, Matthewson.

Autograph please! Jimmy Gemmell signs as requested, watched by Bullock, Chalmers, Matthewson, Clipson and Robbie.

Training 1936 style was obviously a little different to current methods, as trainer Day sets his lads to work on the car park outside the centre-stand. 'Reserved Chairs 2/6d including Tax' states the notice over the turnstile.

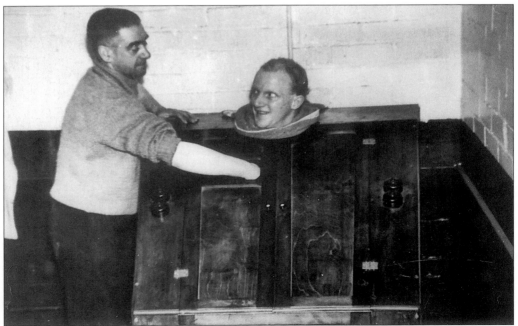

Bury's Bill Gorman takes a steam bath at Gigg Lane, under the guidance of Billy Day – but the contraption looks decidedly unsafe!

The programme cover from Bury's matchday programme of 1938 was a splendid affair, tinted blue and incorporating various action shots, along with a (somewhat inaccurate) artist's impression of Gigg Lane. The whole programme just before the war was a first-class effort, as Bury deliberately sought to increase sales through improved reading matter.

Under the watchful eye of David Robbie, the players enjoy a light jog on Tommy Marshall's pristine pitch in August 1938. Notice the newly-constructed Manchester Road stand in the background. This is not quite finished yet, as the crush barriers lie flat on the terracing and ladders lead precariously to the roof.

Bury's pre-war trainers always enjoyed long associations with the club and Billy Day (left) and Sam Ensor were no exception. Peter Yates was the Shakers' trainer from 1886 until his death in 1904. His son, Alf Yates, succeeded him and remained in the position for more than twenty years. Day, a former reserve outside right between 1908 and 1910, joined as assistant trainer in 1922 and remained until September 1947.

An optical illusion as George Davies becomes a contortionist – the legs actually belong to team-mate Donald Carter. The field is land owned by the club and situated just behind the Cemetery End.

Full-back Bill Gorman joined Bury for a fee of just £75 in September 1934 and gained the first of his eleven international caps for Northern Ireland whilst at the club, albeit even before he made his first team debut for the Shakers. He eventually played fifty-two games for Bury, before moving south to Division One Brentford for £7,000 in December 1938.

The joke appears to be on George Matthewson as the Bury trainer seeks retribution with a little shoe polish – egged on by the other players of course. Despite the year being 1938 and the war looming, it seems there was no problem raising a smile at Gigg Lane.

George Davies is presented with a free header in the 1937/38 season, although the opposition are unknown. Signed for just £20 from Earlstown Bohemians in August 1937, centre forward George was a sensation in his first season at the club, scoring twenty-five goals in just twenty-eight games. A serious knee injury sustained in April 1938 set him back and he was never quite the same player again following the injury.

Three
Forties Boom, Fifties Struggle

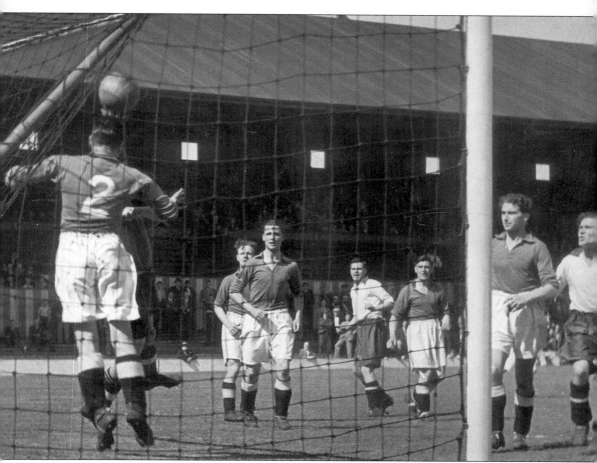

The crowd is sparse in this wartime game at Gigg Lane, thought to be against Everton, as an effort from George Davies (middle of picture) is headed off the line by the full-back.

Wearing grim faces and the uniform of the Bury ARP, Shakers players Jimmy Gemmell and David Robbie fill sandbags during the Second World War.

Manager Norman Bullock, his dog and the Captain, David Jones, welcome the newcomers to Gigg Lane as the players report back for pre-season training in 1946. Tom Peters and David Jones are shaking hands.

Gigg Lane was still considered a very impressive ground in 1946 and was always kept spick and span. Notice the South paddock was just an earth mound (no terracing yet) and sloped down only to pitch level. There is just a wooden fence surrounding the pitch and 'Crown Ales' was the advert on the Manchester Road End, for some two decades, before 'Old Charlie Rum' came along.

Bury embarked on what was only the club's second overseas tour in June 1947 which – like the first tour – took the Shakers to Denmark. Games were played against Esbjerg, Aarhus, Aalborg and a Danish XI and the lads are seen here lining up as they are officially welcomed to Esbjerg.

Fulham 'keeper Ted Hinton gathers the ball safely in their game at Gigg Lane on 13 September 1947. An Eddie Kilshaw goal later beat Hinton to send 14,383 people home very happy.

18 October 1947 and Shakers 'keeper George Bradshaw breaks his leg in this eighth-minute tackle during the game aginst Newcastle at Gigg Lane, with the score at 1-1.

The St John Ambulance men stretcher George off to hospital as team-mates Bill Griffiths, Don Carter, Dave Jones and Reg Halton watch helplessly.

Still with the Newcastle game in October 1947, centre forward Jimmy Constantine took over between the posts and, although he did his best, Bury were well-beaten 5-3.

In March 1948, Bury Football Club purchased Lower Gigg Lane for the first time – which was known at the time as the Christian Sports Ground. It was purchased to give the 'A' team a permanent home and proved to be a sensible acquisition over the years.

Eric Massey scores Bury's opening goal in a 2-0 win against West Ham at a sunny Gigg Lane, in front of a crowd of 23,754. The result gave Bury a four-point lead at the top of Division Two.

Reg Halton shields the ball from former Shaker Bill Gorman, on his return to Gigg Lane on 25 September 1948 with Brentford, when he helped to inflict a 2-1 defeat on his old team.

A George Hazlett cross eludes West Ham 'keeper Gregory in Bury's 3-0 win on 14 October 1950. He is able to recover the ball though, before the on-rushing Harold Bodle can capitalise on his error.

A Tom Daniel shot comes back off the crossbar in a 1-1 draw against Sheffield United at Gigg Lane on 10 March 1951. Unfortunately, Jimmy Greenhalgh was unable to connect with the rebound.

Tom Daniel watches as his seventy-eighth minute shot flies into the top corner of the Nottingham Forest net at Gigg Lane on 13 October 1951. A crowd of 17,007 went home happy, after a 2-0 Shakers' success.

A controversial moment in the same game against Forest, as 'keeper Burgin, under pressure from Bobby Dale, knocks the ball into his own net. Unfortunately, Fletcher's corner had swerved out of play, and a goal kick had already been awarded.

Ken Plant finds little luck in a 1-1 draw against Doncaster Rovers in October 1951, as his shot goes wide of the post.

A sunny summer's day at Gigg Lane in the early 1950s and pre-season training is in full flow with a touch of skipping. Les Hart (middle front) looks unimpressed by it all.

A quiet, traffic-free, cobbled Gigg Lane in March 1951. Notice the goalposts chalked on the wall and advertisements which read 'Fuel Warning. Please be extra careful with coal, electricity, gas. Help to keep the factories working'. There is also a poster stating 'For a man's life with good pay, join the regular army'.

Talent of the future perhaps? A young lad protects his 'goal' on the forecourt in 1951. Notice the advertisements on the main stand, whilst the turnstile prices are 'First team 1/3d Reserves 6d'.

Only eleven people have played more League games for Bury Football Club than Les Hart – and that is despite the war interrupting his Gigg Lane career. Les joined Bury in March 1937 and played twenty-four pre-war games. In post-war times, he increased that total to 280 games, remaining as a player for a total of fifteen years, until hanging his boots up in 1953 and joining the coaching staff. Later becoming the trainer, physiotherapist and even manager at the club, Les personified the spirit of Gigg Lane.

Four of Bury's most loyal post-war players take a breather after training in 1952. Between them, George Griffiths, Cyril Fairclough, Bobby Conroy and Eric Massey amassed 849 League appearances for the Shakers.

Jimmy Greenhalgh beats the Sheffield United defender, but sends his shot crashing against the underside of the crossbar in this game in November 1952. The luck wasn't with Bury, as United triumphed 4-0.

The occasion is the 1952 Club Christmas Party at the Derby Hall and a very smart-looking Bury manager, John McNeil, chats to Les Hart. John McNeil was a player at the club in 1939 and returned in March 1950 to succeed Norman Bullock in the Gigg Lane hot seat.

Congratulations from Doug Fletcher go to twenty-year-old Stuart Imlach on 10 January 1953 for scoring the third goal in a 3-1 away win at Grimsby in the FA Cup Third Round. From left to right: Gleadall, Kelly, Fletcher, Massey, Walton, Daniel, Bardsley, Imlach, Hart, Head, Kirk.

Bury's reward for the victory against Grimsby was a Fourth Round tie at Highbury against Arsenal. The players decided to take a pre-match stroll on the terraces and perhaps pondered their fate – which was a 6-2 thrashing with three goals being conceded in a seven-minute spell.

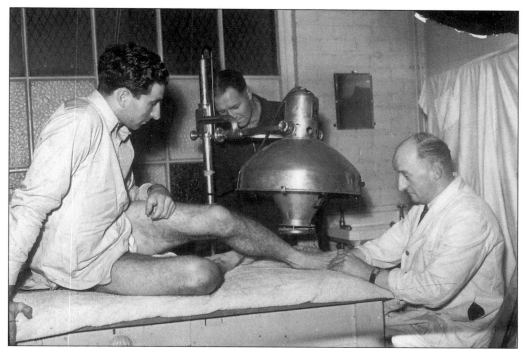

Eric Massey receives treatment on an ankle injury from trainer Hubert Nuttall and his assistant Jack Marshall.

Bury became the first northern club to install floodlighting in October 1953, thanks to the determination of club director Bill Allen. The steelwork was erected by a Bury firm, Joseph Webb & Sons Limited.

OFFICIAL PROGRAMME · · 3ᴰ

BURY

FOOTBALL CLUB

v

WOLVERHAMPTON W.

GIGG LANE · BURY

FIRST FLOODLIGHT GAME

TUESDAY, 6th OCTOBER, 1953

Kick-Off · · 7-45 p.m.

A courageous save is required from Bury 'keeper Chris Conway to keep out the Stoke centre forward, Short, in a 1-1 draw played on 27 December 1954. May and Neilson are the other Bury players in view. The crowd of 24,091 was Bury's second best of the season.

Doug Clarke pulls a good save out of Blackburn 'keeper Elvy at Gigg Lane on 8 October 1955 but, unfortunately, the crowd of 16,946 are disappointed to see Rovers win 4-0.

Hard at work training in 1956 are May, Massey, Neilson, Tilley, Parker and Conroy. The venue is the gym under the Main Stand, which doesn't look to be equipped with many luxury items.

Looking smart in their club blazers, the Bury players are about to leave for a pre-season, three-match tour of Germany in August 1956. However, before the coach can depart, there is a speech from director Tom Kay. Bury played Victoria Berlin (0-3), Spandau (4-3) and Hertha BSC (3-1).

Stan Pearson held, for many years, the distinction of being the oldest-ever player to appear for Bury, at thirty-eight years and 241 days. Scoring fifty-six goals in 121 games for the Shakers, Stan's £4,000 transfer fee proved to be a bargain, despite his age. Here Stan is scoring in Bury's 7-2 win against Bristol Rovers on Christmas Day 1956 – a game in which he grabbed one of his four hat-tricks for Bury. Bruce Grobelaar finally broke Stan's record in 1998.

All aboard for Reykjavik. The Shakers embarked upon a five-match tour of Iceland in June 1958 and, for the first time, chose to travel by aeroplane. Eager to board, 'young' John McGrath is last in line.

Bury FC first decided to fly to selected away League games during the 1959/60 season. The initial flight was to Southampton in October and the Shakers won 2-0. They tried it again the following April, for their away fixture at Bournemouth, but lost that game 2-1. On the way here to Dean Court, vice-chairman Bill Allen (far left) is looking particularly youthful, whilst manager Dave Russell looks very business-like with his briefcase.

A rare visit to Gigg Lane for Stanley Matthews, who is deep in discussion with Les Hart. Manager Dave Russell is able to raise a smile though.

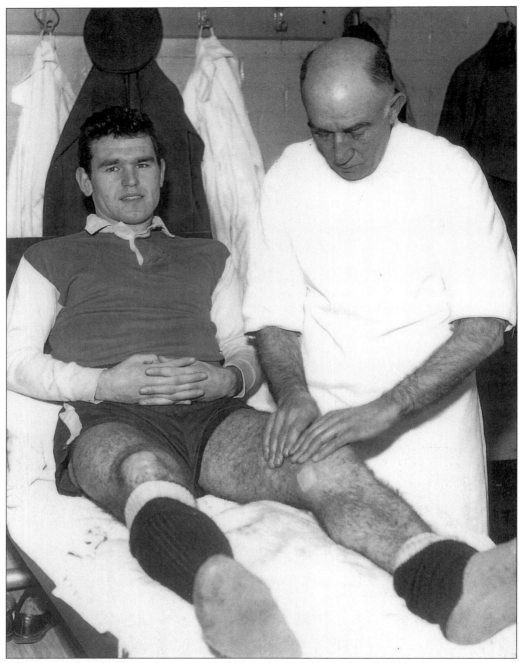

An injury to his left knee takes centre half John McGrath into David Robbie's treatment room during the late 1950s.

Four
Swinging Sixties
– and Seventies

The Manchester Senior Cup is the trophy proudly held by Harry Bunner in March 1960, with Bury having just beaten Oldham 5-1 in the final at Gigg Lane. His team-mates are, from left to right: Neill, Adams, Robertson, Watson, May, Conroy, Bunner, Bradbury, Calder, Lovie and Bartley.

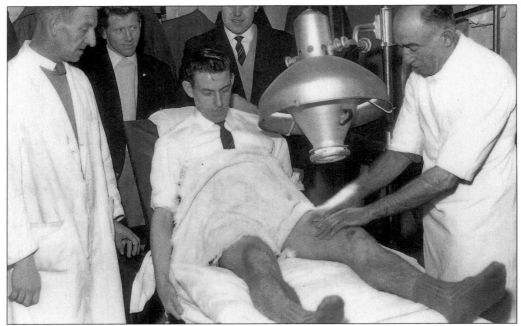

A packed treatment room as David Robbie and Les Hart tend to Frank Adams in 1959. Gordon Atherton and John McGrath look on.

There was a gap of sixty-five years between Bury's first two championship successes. This is the line-up from the 1961 Division Three title-winning team. From left to right, the directors at the back: Russell, Lord, Horridge, Taylor, Austin. Players on back row: Stokoe, Turner, Heath, Hart, Adams, Conroy, Bunner. Middle row: Calder, Holden, Watson, Jackson, Hubbard, Atherton. Front row: Gallagher, McInnes, Robertson, Bartley.

The celebrations begin as Bury win 3-0 against Hull City at Gigg Lane on 22 April 1961 to clinch the Division Three title.

This superb model of Gigg Lane is actually a cake, presented by the supporters' club at their championship celebration dinner in May 1961 at the Co-op Hall. Featured in the photograph are: Bill Calder, Bobby Conroy, H. Coulton (representing the supporters' club), Brian Gallagher, Don Watson, Brian Turner, Gordon Atherton and Johnny Hubbard.

Bill Calder's right boot connects with the ball to score the only goal of the game against Cardiff City on 3 November 1962. He went on to become Bury's leading goalscorer in the 1962/63 season, with eighteen goals.

Colin Bell bursts through to score against Swansea Town in this Division Two fixture, played on 4 September 1964. However, The Swans came back to earn a 2-2 draw.

A young Alec Lindsay (left) and Kevin Randall are watched by trainer Les Hart in 1965. After 126 games for Bury, Lindsay was destined for a £67,000 transfer to Liverpool in March 1969 and a glittering career at the top level, including England international honours. Randall, meanwhile, joined Chesterfield in 1969 and played 258 games for the Spireites.

Bury FC Social Club first opened its doors on 11 December 1965, having cost £40,000 to build. 'It is intended as a meeting place and social centre where people of all ages and tastes may obtain pleasure and comfort in a friendly atmosphere and at the same time stimulate knowledge and interest in and also help to maintain a successful Football League Club', commented Bill Allen, the chairman at the time.

Alf Arrowsmith holds off Derby County's Roy McFarland at a packed Gigg Lane on 25 January 1969. Eventually finishing the season as champions, Derby won 1-0.

Bobby Collins is on the ball against Derby, as Bury attack the Manchester Road End. Notice the old scoreboard, which disappeared not long afterwards.

A Friday evening Bury *v.* Bolton derby game at Gigg Lane on 7 March 1969 and two mounted police keep a watchful eye over the queue for the junior turnstile.

The old turnstiles were introduced back in 1924 and were used right up until 1981, when the need for greater segregation brought changes. There were twenty-four turnstiles in all and you must presume that this photograph was taken early, considering the fact that 11,755 attended the Bolton game.

The Main Stand enclosure was one of the most popular parts of the ground prior to its closure in 1985. This atmospheric view shows part of the crowd for the 1969 derby game against Bolton.

The tension mounts outside the dressing rooms in 1969. This corridor hasn't really changed much almost thirty years later – despite the re-building of the Main Stand.

Another unusual view of the 1969 Bolton game, as Greg Farrell prepares to take a corner.

The excitement of a derby game and the little girl reads her programme whilst the two lads turn away from the action. The policeman doesn't seem to have too many problems to deal with – at least he's following the play!

Norwich City's Geoff Butler sends the ball crashing into his own net after just forty-eight seconds of their Division Two game at Gigg Lane on 22 March 1969. Possibly the fastest own goal for Bury? Wrong – six months later, Brighton's John Napier obliged after thirty-five seconds!

Greg Farrell heads towards the Norwich goal at a seemingly near-deserted Gigg Lane in March 1969.

George Jones' shot is saved by the Huddersfield 'keeper in a 1-1 draw at Gigg Lane in April 1969.

With Bury already relegated, it was of little consequence that they defeated Portsmouth in the final Division Two fixture of the 1968/69 season. Alf Arrowsmith is thwarted here by Pompey 'keeper John Milkins. Ex-Shaker Ray Pointer lurks in the background.

Back in Division Three in August 1969 and Jimmy Kerr is shackled by Brighton defender Bob Smith, who was destined to become the Bury boss four years later.

Brian Turner's 454 League games for Bury places him third in the list of all-time club appearances, behind only Wally Amos and Norman Bullock. Brian was a magnificent servant of the club between 1957 and 1970 and is pictured here assisting the attack in a Division Three game against Barnsley on 13 September 1969.

Jimmy Kerr tucks away a penalty in Bury's FA Cup tie against Mansfield Town in November 1969. The game ended 2-2 and, unfortunately, the Shakers lost the replay.

These likely lads are acting as judges in the Miss Bury FC contest of 1969 and they voted Julie Sylvester the winner. From left to right: Jimmy Kerr, Colin Bell, Colin Waldron, Brian Turner and Joe Mercer (Manchester City Manager).

A diving header from Jimmy Kerr put Bury 4-1 ahead against Stockport County in a Division Three fixture in January 1970. The game also marked Terry McDermott's debut for the Shakers.

Rossendale United and Bolton Wanderers fight out an FA Cup Second Round tie at Gigg Lane in 1971. This was the only use of the ground as a neutral venue until Preston played Stockport at Gigg Lane in August 1994, as Deepdale was still trying to grow some grass after the artificial surface was removed.

George Jones clocks up another goal towards his Bury career total of 114, with a succesful strike in the 3-0 win against Bristol Rovers on 6 March 1971.

George Jones scores the second goal in a 5-1 win against Reading on 6 February 1971. Bury really were a bogey side for the Biscuitmen during the 1960s and 1970s.

Tom White makes no mistake from the penalty spot, as he helps the Shakers on their way to a 2-0 win against Fulham on 20 March 1971.

Tom White celebrates as the ball goes into the net for an own goal from Plymouth's David Provan in April 1971. Bury won 3-0, but would still be relegated.

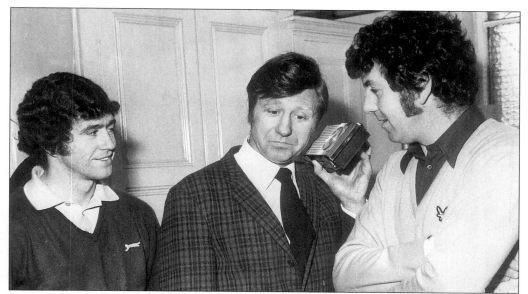

Having beaten Lincoln and Workington in the FA Cup during the 1971/72 season, boss Tom McAnearney listens to the Third Round draw with John Murray and Ken Hancock. Out comes a home tie against Rotherham United – managed by Tom's brother.

The Bury Times attempted to whip up a little FA Cup fever with this photograph in January 1972. A young Terry McDermott is featured (far left), but just twelve months later he was on his way to Newcastle in a £27,000 transfer.

The power crisis of 1974 led to Sunday football for the first time at Gigg Lane and, coupled with continued playing success, led to a big increase in crowds. 8,813 turned up on 17 February to witness an exciting 3-2 win against fellow promotion hopefuls Gillingham. It took a long range shot from Steve Hoolickin (third from right) to secure both points.

The reign of Bill Allen as chairman may have been somewhat controversial, but he certainly ran a tight ship (in every sense of the word) and he always had the good of the club at heart. Bob Smith was only twenty-nine-years old when he was appointed as Bury's youngest-ever manager in December 1973, but he more than justified his chairman's faith.

Derek Spence scored what most Bury fans will remember as the best goal of his career, on 30 March 1974 against Barnsley. A mazy run, two defenders beaten, a one-two with David Howitt and a shot crashed into the roof of the net – a magnificent goal!

A superb ovation for a magnificent goal. Derek Spence milks the adulation – and who could blame him?

Captain Peter Swan (to the right of the flag) is lifted high as the Shakers' supporters celebrate promotion back to Division Three. Bury had just beaten Newport County 5-0 on 27 April 1974 in Swan's last game for the Shakers before leaving the club for Matlock Town. Having been banned from football for seven years, it was a triumphant last season in the Football League for him.

Andy Rowland leaves the Preston defenders floundering, as he puts Bury 2-1 ahead in a League Cup tie in August 1974. Signed earlier that month for £10,000 from Derby, he scored fifty-seven League goals in 162 games and the club eventually made a £78,000 profit when he followed Bob Smith to Swindon in September 1978.

During the 1970s, manager Bob Smith favoured pre-season trips to Scotland. The players are featured here at sunny Troon in July 1975, relaxing before playing warm-up games against Clydebank, St Mirren and Kilmarnock.

Andy Rowland opens the scoring against Tranmere Rovers in a Division Three game, which Bury won 2-1, in September 1976.

Bury's 1903 FA Cup-winning ball stood proudly in a glass case in the Gigg Lane boardroom for two decades, after being presented to the club in 1951. In 1971 it was loaned to a London-based Football exhibition and never returned. A false alarm in 1976 saw groundsman Tommy Marshall and physiotherapist Les Hart (104 years' service to the club between them!) examine the 'wrong' ball. In 1998, it was finally ascertained that the FA now have possession of Bury's beloved ball.

When the slim-line figure of teenage Peter Farrell burst onto the scene in 1976, great things were predicted for the skilful midfielder, but a knee injury disrupted his career at Gigg Lane and he moved on to Port Vale, Rochdale and then Crewe. Peter scored eight goals in his forty-one League games, including this goal against Tranmere in September 1976.

David Gregory cost Bury a record fee of £35,000 when he signed from Stoke City in September 1978. Although the classy striker spent only just over a year with the club, he was very popular, scoring fifteen goals in fifty games – including this strike against Sheffield United in October 1979.

The 1979/80 season brought one long relegation struggle, firstly for Dave Hatton and then for his successor Dave Connor. On the positive side though, Bury enjoyed a good FA Cup run and, after beating Burton, York and Rochdale, a crowd of 17,722 saw Bury dispose of Burnley at Gigg Lane in Round Four. Here, to the backing of a packed stand, John Waddington tidies up in defence.

John Forrest was Bury's last line of defence for fourteen years and the Bury-born 'keeper played in 430 League games for the Shakers, making him, without doubt, one of the club's all-time greats. John collects safely here in the FA Cup tie against Burnley.

The excitement is there for all to see as the crowd erupts on the final whistle, with Bury having beaten Burnley 1-0. Youngsters run to acclaim their heroes. The Shakers are in the Fifth Round of the FA Cup for the first time since 1932.

The celebrations spill over to the dressing room as a Fifth Round tie at Anfield awaits. From left to right: Forrest, Kennedy, Waddington, Wilson, Johnson, McIlwraith, Whitehead, Mullen, Hilton, Constantine, Halford.

The big day arrives and the Bury fans snap up all the available tickets. The scene is set for a possible cup upset – at least 6,500 travelling fans think so!

The Shakers lost 2-0 at Anfield, but gave Liverpool a very tough time along the way and were afforded a standing ovation at the final whistle. Steve Johnson climbs high above Ray Kennedy to get in a firm header.

Five

Eighties Recovery, Nineties Boom

A sad day for Les Hart on 29 March 1980, as Jimmy McIlwraith makes a presentation on behalf of the players to mark the stalwart's retirement after forty-four years at Gigg Lane. To add to the sadness, Bury lost 2-0 to Gillingham!

Gigg Lane is seen here in the summer months of 1980, with few changes evident since the 1920s. The South Paddock has been terraced, the Manchester Road End gained a roof in 1938, floodlights were installed in 1954 and the Cemetery End Stand was added in 1962. The ground contained three wooden stands though and, with wooden terracing at both ends as well, Bury's home quite possibly contained more wood than any other Football League ground.

'David Who?' That was the cry as the Tannoy announced David Bradley at number five in Bury's line-up against Newcastle United in their League Cup Second Round tie in August 1980. Signed the previous day, Bradley (far left) marked his debut by heading the only goal of the game.

The reward – if that is the correct word – for Bradley's goal was a Third Round home tie against European Champions Nottingham Forest. The Shakers lay in ninety-second position in the Football League at the time and Forest tore Bury apart, winning 7-0. A rare Bury attack sees Kenny Burns head clear for a corner under pressure from Steve Johnson.

Steve Johnson grabbed his first-ever Football League hat-trick during Bury's 3-1 win against Rochdale in March 1980. It was a hat-trick with a difference as, on a muddy pitch, the popular Scouse striker scored two penalties and a goal from a couple of inches out after the ball had stuck in the mud.

Paul Hilton celebrates his goal against Bradford City in a 2-2 draw at Gigg Lane on 25 October 1980. Notice the newly-installed gate between the Cemetery End and the car park, as segregation took a hold and the tradition of changing ends finally ceased.

A young Craig Madden celebrates the fourteenth League goal of his career for Bury against Port Vale in September 1980, on his way to becoming the club's record goalscorer with 129 League goals between 1978 and 1986.

Defender Steve Kenworthy is carried off with a broken leg in a match against Colchester United in October 1982. In four consecutive home games, Bury had Kenworthy, Cruickshank, Firth and Hilton carried off. All except Firth missed the remainder of the season, a factor that contributed greatly (especially the loss of Hilton) to the Shakers eventually missing out on promotion on the final day of the season.

Stuart Parker scores the only goal of the game in a 1-0 win against Colchester in October 1982. The other Bury players are Paul Hilton and John Bramhall.

There are twelve men between Tommy Gore and the goalkeeper, but the midfield man still manages to find a gap with this free-kick and open the scoring in Bury's 3-2 win against Chester in March 1983.

Craig Madden heads Bury's goal in the 2-1 Milk Cup defeat against West Ham at Gigg Lane, but there is worse to come in the second leg, as the Shakers go down to a record 10-0 defeat.

Terry Robinson succeeded Ron Clarke as chairman in January 1983 and was able to negotiate the club's first-ever shirt sponsorship deal for the start of the 1984/85 season. 'Spray Breaker' was emblazoned across the Shakers' shirts for just one season and the chairman is featured at the launch with Geoff France from manufacturers Boydell and Jacks.

Craig Madden shows his delight upon scoring his second goal in Bury's 4-2 win against Colchester United in October 1984.

Leighton James was one of Martin Dobson's first signings in August 1984, from Sunderland, and perhaps also one of the most important. Only at Gigg Lane for one season, the Welsh winger was an inspiration during the 1984/85 season, playing in all forty-six League games, scoring five goals and supplying the ammunition for many, many more. Here, he dances past Hereford full-back Ian Bray.

Bury-born Wayne Entwistle, the only man to spend three separate spells as a player with the club, volleys a spectacular goal in Bury's 3-0 win against Tranmere Rovers on 29 December 1984. The Rovers 'keeper is ex-Shaker John Platt.

Following this successful penalty-winner from Trevor Ross against Blackpool in March 1985, ugly scenes arose as hooligans in the sizeable away contingent began to rip out bench seats and dismantle wooden panels in the Main Stand and Cemetery End. The game attracted the biggest crowd of the season (7,978) as the two promotion contenders met head on.

In his first full season at the club, Martin Dobson – and his assistant Frank Casper – guided Bury to promotion back to Division Three, despite a shoe-string budget. Staying clear of injuries, Dobson utilized just sixteen players during 1984/85 – the least number ever used in a single season. The players celebrate after the home game against Wrexham in May 1985.

The repercussions of the Bradford disaster in May 1985 had immediate and far-reaching consequences at Gigg Lane. The Boys' Stand (above) was demolished and the massive wooden Main Stand (below) had its capacity slashed from 5,600 to just 1,600, despite the installation of ten new emergency exits along the front of the stand.

Craig Madden leaps to head home Winston White's cross in Bury's 4-2 win against local rivals Bolton Wanderers at Burnden Park in August 1985. Trotters 'keeper Simon Farnworth also conceded another goal to Madden, just one minute later.

With Gigg Lane's capacity slashed to 8,000 after the Bradford fire, a Milk Cup Second Round tie against Manchester City in September 1985 saw the Shakers utilise Old Trafford as their 'home' venue. A crowd of 11,377 saw City triumph 2-1, with Bury's goal coming from this Trevor Ross penalty.

Martin Dobson became Bury's player/manager in March 1984 and enjoyed much success during his six years in charge, also gaining a reputation for encouraging his players to adopt a neat, attractive passing game. Here, Winston White and Craig Madden celebrate Dobson's penalty success in a 3-0 win against table-toppers Reading in October 1985.

The Shakers lost 4-1 against Bristol City at Ashton Gate in February 1986, but the game marked a personal landmark for striker Craig Madden, who notched a record-breaking 125 goals for the club with this left-foot strike.

Having beaten Chester City, Tranmere Rovers, Barnsley and Reading in the FA Cup in the 1985/86 season, the Shakers made a rare appearance in the Fifth Round stage. Drawn away against Division One Watford, John Bramhall's header earned a creditable 1-1 draw, but Graham Taylor's men were too strong in the replay at Gigg Lane, winning 3-0.

Lee Dixon fires home Bury's fourth goal in a 4-1 win against Blackpool in April 1985. He is being shadowed by future Shaker Colin Greenall.

A relieved-looking Terry Robinson is pictured here, immediately after Bury's 0-0 draw against Brentford in May 1986 had secured the club's Division Three status. Lee Dixon (right) had just been crowned 1985/86 player of the season, with new defender Peter Valentine earning the runners-up award.

Promising youngster David Lee scores his very first senior goal in Bury's Freight Rover Trophy game at Carlisle United in December 1986.

A run in the Littlewoods Cup during the 1987/88 season brought victories against Preston, Sheffield United and QPR. The reward was a Fourth Round fixture, on 18 November, against Manchester United, which was switched from Gigg Lane to Old Trafford on police advice. 8,000 travelling Shakers saw Jamie Hoyland put Bury into a fifty-second minute lead with this shot, but United came back to record a fortunate 2-1 victory.

There was a sweet return to Burnden Park for former Bolton striker Steve Elliott on 12 November 1988, when he scored twice in Bury's 4-2 win against his former club. This is Steve's second strike against the Wanderers.

Liam Robinson scored eighty-nine goals in 262 League games for the Shakers and proved to be a bargain capture, having arrived from Huddersfield in June 1986. This thirty-yard strike against Fulham on 28 December 1988 was up amongst his best goals for Bury.

Sam Ellis succeeded Martin Dobson as Bury boss in June 1989 and was immediately given previously unprecedented transfer funds by owner Hugh Eaves, in order to build a side that would take Bury back into Division Two. He was well on his way to achieving that aim, when a subsequent cash crisis in November 1990 led to the squad being dismantled and Ellis moving on to Manchester City. From left to right: Mandy Johnson, Andy Feeley, Sam Ellis, Mike Walsh.

Bury Reserves competed in the Central League for seventy-two years without a hint of a championship, yet the Midland Senior League title was captured, at only the second attempt, in the 1990/91 season. From left to right, back row: Pollitt, Emmett, Bennett, Atkin, Dunn, Simms. Front row: Greenhalgh, Kent, Price, Anderson, Bradley.

Jamie Hoyland looks serious, even though his goal has just put Bury 2-0 ahead against Bolton Wanderers on 24 April 1990 and guaranteed the Shakers a place in the play-offs. Liam Robinson is about to offer his congratulations.

David Lee confidently bangs home a penalty on his way to a hat-trick in Bury's 3-1 win against Cambridge United in March 1991. Lee really was in his best form at the time and it was only another five months before a fee of £400,000 took him to Southampton.

Gigg Lane was used as the setting for a scene from a BBC TV programme called *A Likely Lad* on 3 October 1991. The club's apprentices were used as extras and were decked out accordingly in Victorian costumes. Can you spot future first-team players Ian Hughes and Lee Anderson?

A powerful header from Kevin Hulme gives the Bolton-born striker a goal during a rare Bury defeat at Burnden Park (2-1) in March 1992.

Ian Stevens watches the ball hit the back of the net as he records a hat-trick in Bury's 4-2 win against Leyton Orient in February 1992.

This is what the Main Stand looked like on 17 June 1992, as the ground redevelopment finally got underway. All the wood, along with the tarred roof, was removed and a new structure built upon the original 1924 steel framework.

Swinton Rugby League Club moved in as tenants at Gigg Lane for the first time in 1992, as the Shakers sought to maximise use of the new facilities at the stadium. Swinton played the first game at their new home on 30 August and began with a 10-14 defeat against Rochdale Hornets in front of a crowd of 1,803.

Nigerian international David Adekola burst onto the scene during the 1992/93 campaign. His boot goes flying as he sends his eighth goal of the season past Halifax Town 'keeper Lee Bracey.

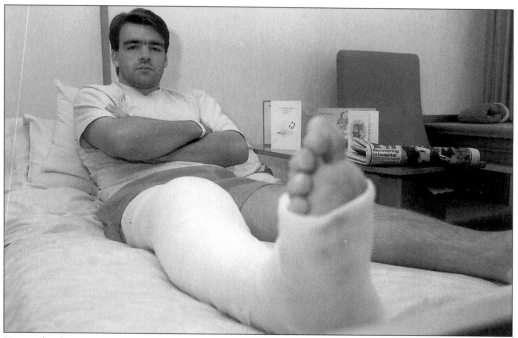

His right leg in plaster, goalkeeper Gary Kelly's season was ended in August 1993 after a dreadful challenge from Bolton's John McGinlay in a Coca-Cola Cup tie at Burnden Park.

Undoubtedly Mike Walsh's most inspired signing, Chris Lucketti, arrived as a replacement for Alan Knill in September 1993 from Halifax Town. The £50,000 fee has been re-paid time and time again, as Chris helped Bury climb up through the divisions and it now seems a very long time since he scored his first League goal for the club against Doncaster in January 1994. Notice Mark Carter is wearing number twenty-one, in the only season that Bury used squad numbers.

The South Stand begins to take shape in March 1994, as the Gigg Lane revolution continues. The stand is officially 'opened' for a Lancashire Cup game against Manchester United in July 1994, although it was also used prior to this for the Lacrosse World Cup Finals held in the same summer.

Master craftsman! Mark Carter hit forty-two goals in his three seasons at Gigg Lane, following his £6,000 transfer from Barnet in September 1993 and was leading scorer in both the 1995/96 promotion season and the 1996/97 championship season.

David Pugh bangs home a forty-first minute goal to give Bury a 1-0 lead at Deepdale against Preston North End in the play-off semi-final. The Shakers finish off the job and reach Wembley, courtesy of a similar 1-0 success in the second leg at Gigg Lane.

The Shakers look pensive as they take the field at Wembley on 27 May 1995 for the play-off final against Chesterfield.

Chris Lucketti gets in a powerful header against Chesterfield at Wembley.

Disappointment is etched on the faces of Hugh Eaves, Nev and Jill Neville and Terry and Brenda Robinson, as David Pugh leads the players up to the royal box at Wembley, following their 2-0 defeat against Chesterfield.

There are tears from Phil Stant as the players are consoled by the Shakers' supporters on their way back down onto the Wembley pitch.

Twelve months after the Wembley heartache and Bury are promoted automatically in May 1996. Everyone was determined to enjoy the occasion. From left to right: Pugh, Daws, Johnson, Rigby, Woodward, Bimson, Cross, Kelly, West, Lucketti, Stant.

The Shakers' fans had waited quite some time for a knees-up and had to wait a little bit longer before they were finally able to celebrate in May 1996, after Bury had beaten Cardiff 3-0 in the final game of the season. The celebrations began though once news came through of Darlington's failure to win at Scunthorpe in a game that had kicked-off late.

'Well Done Shakers' says the banner (in May 1996) which was acquired by the local council to celebrate anticipated success twelve months earlier at Wembley. The council got good use out of the banner over the next few years though, as the fans almost came to expect an annual civic reception!

A superb goal from Lennie Johnrose as the ball flies into the top corner after just fourteen minutes against Preston North End in December 1996. This win took the Shakers into third place in Division Two.

Needing a point for promotion to Division One, there are just three minutes remaining when lines-person Wendy Toms signals for a Watford penalty in Bury's game at Vicarage Road on 26 April 1997. Disaster was averted though, as hero Dean Kiely saves Tommy Mooney's spot-kick and the Shakers players and their large travelling contingent of fans can begin celebrating promotion following the 0-0 draw.

The players continue the celebrations in the Vicarage Road dressing room at the beginning of a very long evening!

Stan Ternent completely turned the club around during his three years in charge at Gigg Lane. He took Bury from twenty-first in Division Three in October 1995 to seventh in Division One in September 1997 and established the Shakers in a safe final position of nineteenth in Division One, before moving on to Burnley. As the only man to guide Bury Football Club to two promotions, he is undoubtedly amongst the most successful managers in the club's history.

The Division Two championship was clinched at Gigg Lane with a 2-0 win against Millwall on 3 May, when around 2,000 people were locked out of the ground. The party atmosphere prevalent on that particular afternoon will never be forgotten by those who were present.

A championship at last – after a thirty-seven year wait. From left to right, back row: Ternent, Ellis, Carter, Battersby, Hughes, Butler, Armstrong, West, Kiely, Rigby, Woodward, O'Kane, Raw. Front row: Dawson, Randall, Daws, Pugh, Lucketti, Johnrose, Jepson, Johnson.

Who could possibly begrudge these two gentlemen their moment of success? Chairman Terry Robinson has worked tirelessly, for nearly two decades, to turn the club around and rebuild the stadium, whilst owner Hugh Eaves provided the finances to keep the club going through some very dark days and has injected a massive amount of money over the past fourteen years. Bury's history has thankfully seen numerous such characters over the past 113 years – Hamer, Bradley, Duckworth, Dean, Horridge and Allen, to name but a few.